Declutter Workbook

A Beginner Guide to Organizing your House, Managing Spaces and Reduce Stress Easily and Effortlessly with Little Secrets to Simplify your Home Life

Dana Leary

© Copyright 2020-2021 by Dana Leary - All rights reserved.

This eBook is provided with the sole purpose of providing relevant information on a specific topic for which every reasonable effort has been made to ensure that it is both accurate and reasonable. Nevertheless, by purchasing this eBook you consent to the fact that the author, as well as the publisher, are in no way experts on the topics contained herein, regardless of any claims as such that may be made within. As such, any suggestions or recommendations that are made within are done so purely for entertainment value. This is a legally binding declaration that is considered both valid and fair by both the Committee of Publishers Association and the American Bar Association and should be considered as legally binding within the United States.

The reproduction, transmission, and duplication of any of the content found herein, including any specific or extended information will be done as an illegal act regardless of the end form the information ultimately takes. This includes copied versions of the work both physical, digital and audio unless express consent of the Publisher is provided beforehand. Any additional rights reserved.

TABLE OF CONTENT

DESCRIPTION

The book is a comprehensive guide to help you clean up the excess mess from your home, office, laptop, garage, etc. We all know that the cleaning procedure is the most difficult job on this planet, but it can't be avoided. Indeed, if you stay messy all the time, you will feel low and will not be able to perform with your utmost capability and capacity. This book wants to encourage you and help you to bring cleanliness not within your home, but within yourself too.

The book talks about the effect and benefits of decluttering your house. It provides facts and evidence to the reader, to encourage them to perform decluttering at their workplace, home, and different messy places. It also provides the benefits of productivity that can be achieved with decluttering. Apart from this, the book mentions different quotes from famous personalities that encourage people to have a decluttering habit.

This is not all, the book talks about the effect of decluttering on cognitive abilities. People tend to perform way better when their desks are neat and tidy. On the other hand, the memory of the person is also improved. You will be able to manage your time more efficiently and effectively.

The book talks about room-by-room decluttering. In this, the book provides different tips and tricks to remove the unnecessary material from the portions of your house. The portions are highlighted to help you read more effectively. It also talks about different rescue services that can help you in decluttering. In today's world, keeping yourself neat and tidy can save you from many diseases.

"You'll never get organized if you don't have a vision for your life." –Linda L.EuBanks.

INTRODUCTION

"Once we give up being attached to physical possession, we find the time and freedom to follow bigger dreams." –Joshua Becker.

Decluttering is very necessary. It just keeps your mind, soul, and body active and fresh. You have to learn the power to get rid of excessive or wasteful material from your life. This act will always lower your burden and will bring ease in your lifestyle. Imagine, getting rid of all the negativity on your way to success. Only thinking about it brings so much peace and calm, however, imagine the fun in achieving it. Therefore, this guide will provide you a way to declutter the unnecessary stuff.

The first and most important thing is the mindset. You need to have a positive mindset and attitude to achieve the goal that you desire. If you are working half-heartedly, there is a very low chance of winning. You will not be able to get rid of your cluttered stuff. This will always bring hindrance in your life. Always have a growth mindset this will boost up your learning abilities and cognitive potential.

Imagine, you visit a friend of yours after a long time. You see that his house is entirely messed up and there is no place to breathe. What will this leave an impression on you? Of course, you will consider your friend as immature, irresponsible, and dirty. You might feel irritated or feel disrespectful. All these reactions are possible. In the workplace, the employees should keep their desks clean at all times. This leaves a very positive and powerful impression on the boss. Moreover, having a clean and organized laptop saves you lots of time. Want to know how? Well, imagine that your boss asks for a file that is somewhere on your laptop. If you have an organized document folder, you will send the file in no time and without any stress or tension. However, on the other hand, if you have a messed up situation, you will not be able to send the document on time and this will leave a highly negative impression on your boss.

Furthermore, nothing is greater than mental health and peace. If you are stressed all the time, and you don't have a healthy or clean place to retire. This will cause an effect on your mental ability, performance, socialization, and more.

Think for a second that you came back home from work, all tired and exhausted, and saw a messy home ahead. You will be devastated. You will become even more tired. This sounds bad, and indeed, it is bad.

Decluttering of house, offices, workplace, etc. is very important and should be given proper thought. This book is a comprehensive guide to help the reader in decluttering their places. Let's happily declutter our houses!

CHAPTER ONE: HOW DECLUTTERING BRINGS HAPPINESS & CALMNESS

De-cluttering is the removal of unnecessary items from private places and public places that are untidy and overcrowded. There are a lot of things to enjoy, to bring happiness, to bring yourself at ease and calm and de-cluttering is one of them and the most significant one as well. It is not limited to the concept of physical space but also we can relate it to mental health as well. When we get both the things done together, then they start increasing our focus and free our minds to get things done with no stress and enjoy life along the way. So cluttering can be something physical like books and clothes with mental and emotions in advance. Everyone should notice that a cluttered mind remains multidirectional and little things get done because his vision gets blurred and cloudy as compared to other people who remain sharp just because they don't have a problem as such. We can de-clutter the things in different manners like we can de-clutter our friends, we can de-clutter our commitments, our work area, our computer, home, office and so much more.

People get late or constantly unprepared, often stressed, no matter it might be some other reason, but their cluttered mind most probably and they wander here and there to get things done, they struggle to find items when they need them, they place them and immediately forget that where they placed the item prior and comes in anger which results in dangerous things like they bash on their families like brothers, sisters, wife, and even parents and it is said that in such cases usually, they get responsible because they usually place their items and think that some other member of the family placed it somewhere and shout on them. Disorganization usually comes from a lot of physical and mental clutter and they are usually their attachments, fears, old letters or clothes. It is said that the amount of stress the families experience at home varies directly to the amount of stuff they usually possess. Things or we can say them items which include our clothes, shoes, papers, school bags, books, like from pen and pencil to the large items that we usually possess like party suits, ties, pictures, kitchen items like our grocery, etc. These are directly involved in a person's life, they affect the mood, self-esteem, they show that how responsible and caring the person is, how well he organizes his items at home, school, office or any other place of to live.

Virtually every residence can benefit in some way to improve. Although there is nothing exterior about the appearance of the room, there are always steps that can be taken to make the best use of its space. There are a lot of ideas that we can use them to set our room and maximize the spaces and make it more presentable in general. Pursuing a sense of harmony between yourself and your home or apartment offers many psychological benefits for scientific reasons. Whether it means dumping half of your belongings or - in the case of highly sensitive, functional or financial value - moving elsewhere, the diversion process is likely to lead to improvement.

Our happiness and calmness depend upon how distressful we are. Stress makes our life very hard to live in. After all, you are bound to something that resists you to do a particular thing that appeals to you but makes sure it is more positive because something can be more negative that is appealing to us but unacceptable in the society. But we want to know that how de-clutter reduces stress level so if we take an example of being overweight we get to know that Being overweight is often a symptom and cause of stress and can affect every aspect of your life: from the time you take things to your finances and the enjoyment of everything in life. Clutter can distract you, make you lose weight and often invites chaos in your life which results in stress. Blending can seem like an undeniable task if you don't know where to start or how to start. By spending less of your time clearing your life and keeping things tidy, you will reap the benefits of comfortable living spaces, reduced stress, and an organized and impactful presence.

We can make ourselves happier and calm if we de-clutter our lives. First of all, we can reduce our commitments. Commitments that we usually have of our schools, offices, our home, our hobbies like if someone likes to do sketching then he spends all of the time in sketching then we can reduce the time that our work is consuming, there are many other commitments that we have like with our friends for example if we have to reach somewhere in time them or we have made promises to them that we must have to fulfill even if it could be difficult for us as well. Examine every area of your life and write down your commitments. Seeing all of this written down can be overwhelming with a lot of eye-opening experience. From here, look at everything and decide if it brings you joy and value, and whether the time you invest in it is worth it. Another way to reduce your commitments is to find some that you like and get rid of the rest. Learn how to say no and turn down offers. If you get rid of the ones that don't bring you joy or value, you'll have more time for the things you love. If we reconsider the routines that we are used to and try to de-clutter the useless commitments, then this will help us a lot if we do care. Most of us do not have periods spent in our daily lives and simply deal with our obligations, chores and daily chores. Without a building, it can lead to days of chaos and productivity decline. Batch tasks together. Instead of washing your clothes several times a week, do it all in one day. It helps to document all your weekly and daily obligations, tasks, and schedule daily and weekly guidelines. Grab it where you can see it and try to follow it. You may find that being proactive brings a new sense of peace and order to your life. When we talk about people then we should consider as much positivity as possible. We have those people who want to live their life permanently with you. Your best friend usually comes in this category but still, it varies. Maybe you consider him/her your best friend but he doesn't. But we are here to discuss more positively. We also pass by toxic people in our lives who always want to make us feel bad, stops us to do anything better for ourselves, for other people, etc. we should avoid them as much as possible because they are not with you for you but they are with you to make you feel bad as much. Then there come temporary people who want to live with you but temporarily and after some time they will go then you both will never meet each other as you were used to. To de-clutter your friendship is a very effective idea because it will reduce the commitments we have with friends, it will save our time, it will save us from toxic people. I always suggest that have friends but less and make your selves selective than welcoming everyone to be a part of your list. Quality matters more than quantity and its very common that quality always defeats quantity and you can relate it to other things as well and we should spend more time with positive people, people who help us grow and make us feel happy. The de-cluttering of friends is difficult but it is important and significant. We can embrace labeling a friendship that will help you in finding true friends, understanding the bad connections and avoiding them, label the pseudo good connections and then move towards the real connections that are most important. When you control your environment, you manipulate your life. If you domesticate the fine friendships in your life, you will keep a higher pleasant of existence all around. It is also connected to the relationship life. Difficult to accept, but genuine.

One ponders found that when connections are strained due to contentions over such things as cluttered spaces, the disorganization closes up influencing your life more than it ought to. Clashes of this kind can have an unfavorable impact on your relationship life. You're plenty extra likely to reach your goals since the effect of the humans you spend the most time which shapes your mindset more than you think. People who encourage you, aid you and see the excellent in you will consciously and subconsciously drive you towards what you favor in lifestyles and you'll, in the end, acquire more. By slicing out poisonous relationships, you will begin to see a large distinction in yourself and how you see the world around you in a greater nice light. Don't underestimate what an actual pal can carry to the table.

An RFASR formula is very useful in regards to the concept of de-cluttering:

- Recency – "When did I last use this?"

- Frequency – "Exactly how often do I use this?"
- Acquisition cost – "How expensive and/or difficult is it to get this?"
- Storage cost – "How much does it cost me to store this?"
- Retrieve cost – "What will it cost me if this item becomes outdated, or I need to retrieve it from storage?"

Let's see in some cases to understand this RFASR formula. Assume you've got two lawnmowers in your carport, despite the truth you simply have a small yard. Centering on one lawnmower, in particular, you figure merely last used it months prior (Recency), you have got as it was utilized it around once a year (Frequency), it isn't difficult to purchase modern lawnmowers (Procurement took a toll), putting away it costs you in terms of space (Capacity fetched), and repairing it'll be a bother with in the future since it is very an ancient demonstrate (Recover taken a toll). Hence, you choose to urge freed of it.

Once we have effectively de-cluttered, whether it be one zone or all the regions said over, clutter will start to crawl back into our life. You must be careful in weeding it out on a normal premise, or it'll fair take over our lives once more. Look at the way that we simply do things and how things make their way into our life, and consider whether we will put together a basic framework for everything, from our clothing to work ventures and email. Write down our frameworks step-by-step and attempt to take after them as best as we will. Take after our frameworks and we will keep the clutter minimized.

De-cluttering has a connection with eating as well. Agreeing to The American Affiliation for Nurture Anesthetists, individuals with muddled homes are a whopping 77 percent more likely to be overweight or obese. Peter Walsh's book Lose the Clutter, Lose the Weight builds a strong case for the association between having a domestic full of superfluous clutter and a kitchen full of unfortunate nourishments. This leads to a negative insides monolog that ambushes you as before long as you walk through the entryway – sentiments of depletion and contemplations of not knowing where to start. It's a line of considering that proposes them encompassing the relationship between mental and physical wellbeing less sadness and uneasiness lead to a more advantageous body, and vice-versa. Decluttering can also improve the digestive tract.

Organizing the space can result in the vanishing of side effects like bloating, reflux, destitute absorption, and inflammation. This can be ascribed to the gut-brain association: as your stretch levels diminish and your intellect gets to be less cluttered, your body has more vitality and less oxidative stretch. Your detoxification forms work well, and your microflora is in adjust — all those exquisite supplements you're putting into your body are absorbed and conveyed to the correct put. Our antioxidant security will moreover at that point progress.

There is a syndrome that is not much common, but in the syndrome, there is this fear in the heart that if you see some de-cluttered stuff around you, you think about all the possibilities of mishappening. For example, if you see a sock cluttered near you on the floor, you might think that you will slip over the sock and you will break one of your bones.

There is this myth too that left-handed people are bad at de-cluttering while right-handed people like to stay organized and clean. Well, it always depends on the personal liking and disliking your environment, but in general no, one would like to live in a messy room. Everyone does care about their surroundings and environment and it is known to all that living in a messy room or place lowers your thinking capabilities and brain capacity.

Clutter makes us feel stressed out and exhausted. When everything is spilled away in the room and nothing is looking clean then your OCD (obsessive-compulsive disorder) can get triggered and you will not feel well until you have removed that clutter from that specific place. Wherever you go you will carry the thought of how the clutter is making the place look so disturbing and not organized.

The clutter hides dirt, mold and decaying things under itself. It might result in a smelly place which will be unbearable to live. It will remain in hiding unless the clutter is removed to make it visible and then clean it. Germs also come to such decaying places. They prefer to warn and moisty places to reproduce with some sugar content in them. This can also lead to various health issues. Your body and mind both know this and you will not take a breath of relief unless you de-clutter and clean the place. A de-cluttered room will be more airy and hygienic than the cluttered room. You can replace your clutter with some fresh plants and it will give you a better and healthy feeling. You will have more space for sunshine and a brighter room.

You can not stay happy in a place where you realize from every gaze you give that you have incomplete and pending tasks left around you. How you even sleep properly if that is the case? Clutter reflects that you have a bad mood and you are not in the mood to de-clutter all the stuff. Or you have to do some pending work but you were too tired to do that and you left it in between which leaves you with the clutter of that work too. Now when you leave pending work, your brain lingers on to the thought of pending work because everywhere you look you will be reminded of your unfinished chores and responsibilities. You need to get rid of such clutter as soon as possible. De-cluttering in such cases will not only take away the tension of incomplete work but also de-clutter side by side. You will complete your tasks and given responsibilities and you will not have to worry about your responsibilities.

When you have a lot of de-cluttering to do then there is a high possibility of you breaking your valuables yourself. When there will be clutter it will cover things which are valuable for you and sometimes many expensive ones too. Once you decide to move from one place to another you will have to watch your every step so nothing breaks if you step on it. Moreover, even if you start de-cluttering your clutter and start completing your tasks then you will get tired after some time and you will not be as careful as you were at the start of de-cluttering because you want your things to be done quickly. In these swift moves, you might trip over your things or stepping on them and end up breaking them.

In this busy world, we do not have much time to take note of things and remember where we placed it. When you de-clutter you will have an organized and better room. Your room will transform from a place where you even used to struggle to find a place to put a glass to a well-organized room where you can keep things and stay tension free that you will always find the specific thing in the designated place.

I can conclude surely that de-cluttering is one of the best ways to keep ourselves happier, healthier and calm as never before.

CHAPTER TWO: ROOM-BY-ROOM DECLUTTER

Rooms are considered as a private place as they are a part of our home and home is a private thing. Cluttered life makes a lot of uneasiness and discomfort in life and we are usually not able to live it through full enjoyment and by working according to our interests. Our home provides us that comfort that no other place able to provide it. We must encourage ourselves to take control of our home by showing our best interest and best way to organize, clean and store the items, and considering all the rooms of the house to de-clutter every week. We've already seen de-cluttering guides for the hallway, kitchen, and front room, and now the space we sleep in is within the spotlight, with advice to assist us to achieve a clean, clutter-free and organized bedroom.

Why do we bother de-cluttering so much? This is just because we want to check the possibilities like Is this thing something I frequently use? For example, Once you begin considering approximately your reply, other questions will emerge. You'll begin to consider whether you really utilize the thing on a customary premise, once you another anticipate to require it, whether it takes up a part of time or space, and whether it can be effortlessly supplanted. For illustration, you might have acquired a moderate cooker to utilize it to create supper a few evenings a week, but at that point pushed it to the back of the pantry and overlooked almost it. In case it is fair sitting there, taking up valuable cabinet space, why hold onto it? It's time to say goodbye. if we take another example like Another common illustration like clothing. Most of us are blameworthy of holding onto a dress that doesn't fit us, aren't in design anymore, or fair doesn't fit with our way of life. For occurrence, if you utilized to work in an office but have gone through the final few a long time raising your children full-time, you don't get to keep those keen suits that have been gathering tidy in your closet. If you select to go back to work in an office environment, it's simple to purchase a few of modern suits. Don't let assumptions abrogate your judgment. Some other possibilities are like If not, is this something that I adore and flashes joy? Could somebody else utilize it more than me? Can I get absent without having this in my life? When was the final time I utilized this? Am I keeping this out of commitment or expectation? Am I holding onto this since I think I ought to adore it? Am I sparing this fair in case I'll require it… sometime in the not so distant future, down the road? Do I have products of the same thing? Could something else I claim do the same work? Am I holding onto a broken thing to settle "someday?" Is this thing worth the time I spend cleaning/storing it? Could I utilize this space for something else? What's the most noticeably awful that may happen on the off chance that I get freed of it? Am I putting this within the garbage drawer since it doesn't have a place… or a genuine reason? When getting freed of overabundance clutter, we got to make a choice (or decision) of where that thing will go. When you're learning the method of how to de-clutter your domestic, it is essential to set yourself up for success. This challenge, when utilized suitably, will energize you to require on the tasks to reduce clutter & include organization to your domestic. Think of it as the additional inspiration that you just got to free your domestic of chaos, ease your intellect and put stretch behind you. If you've pondered how to organize your domestic, this challenge will assist you in making choices and wrap up with positive steps taken, without looking like a tornado fair went through your house. When de-cluttering, it is imperative to sort your things and after that choose if you wish to give or hurl them. Take a see at the taking after six categories where each question may go.

It's common for the bedroom to grow to be a dumping ground for laundry, unpacked bags, and unnecessary items. These things show our irresponsibility, our ignorance and our immaturity and disorganization. These are the problems which make our mind to remain disorganized as well. It is not a place of visitors, it is our private place but at this stage, we let clutter accumulate. It is a peaceful place where we should relax and sleep and other items should be kept low in volume. Fewer items will make our room more clean and presentable and more relaxing with a clean environment and the stuffiness will also be very much less as compared to a cluttered one. Keep the item in the same room or put them in another room or what we can do more is we can sell them or give away, try to destroy, recycle or repurpose as well. So, there are a lot of possibilities to approach.

We can reduce the stuffiness of our rooms even if it's a structure like windows, doors are not designed that well. The very first step to maintain from having a stuffy room is to straighten up the room. Take the time to examine the walls, furnishings pictures and so on to see if there is any mold or mildew, which surely generates the musty smell. Mildew and mold can grow exceptionally much anywhere. After straightening up we can also vacuum the floor. This will assist put together for a later, more in-depth cleaning. Rent a steam cleaner or carpet shampooer   from your nearby branch or domestic enhancements stor e.   Clean everywhere in   the   room and under each piece of furniture to make sure that you have cleaned the carpets. Doing this additionally helps to minimize the danger of mold and mildew from the carpets. Remove all the extra bedding, pillows, drapes and curtains from the bedroom or place them somewhere like in a closet. We can also clean the wastebaskets. It may additionally not appear like it however even   the lightest type of bedroom garbage can add to any odors or mustiness in a room. If you do have wastebaskets   in   the   room,   then doing something as simple as a periodic scrubbing will keep down the odors that can accumulate in a bedroom. The quality of air can also be improved by de-cluttering. The different belonging that lies scattered over your house continually collect tidy particles. This increments the sum of poisons and other contaminants coasting through the discussion around you. And this, in turn, leads to hacking, asthma assaults and eye bothering, among other undesirable responses. Freeing your domestic of clutter implies either disposing of these dust-collecting things, cleaning and organizing them or putting them in boxes or other shapes of capacity — or, most likely, a few combinations of these approaches. This speaks to an awfully real step toward more advantageous living. You may be (truly) breathing simpler, not fair since you're less on the edge and unfocused, but since the quality of the indoor discusses itself has progressed.

After removing the stuffiness, then move to the simplification of the rooms. Rooms are usually cluttered in a common house. in case your room is as well cluttered, you'll need to rearrange them. It will save you time in the future because you will feel messy and reluctant to do the task that you are used to doing every day. Doing the same things every day also makes people angry and messed up. Start by clearing off anything that's on the floors. Toss out or give unused things. After clearing the floor, move to level surfaces such as countertops, racks, tops of dressers, etc. clear them as much as possible and after that move onto the furniture. Consider in case you wish everything. Sort things in heaps, hurl, give, or keep. Organize everything that you've chosen to keep into drawers, cabinets, and closets, keeping them out of locating, but still flawlessly organized and uncluttered. Do this one room at a time. Tackling the closet is another big task and quite reluctant but it is what it is. Closets are awesome to put or to store things simply don't need out within the open, and can effortlessly get to be a put where you push things fair to keep them out of view. Go through your closets – take everything out, clean it, and hurl, give as much as you'll be able. Decide a particular put to store anything you choose to keep. Keep as it were the things that we just. cherish and utilize habitually. As for our dress, get freed of anything that we simply haven't worn in six months. Now and then indeed the thought of cleaning out the clutter sounds like an overpowered, on edge errand, but we are going keep it basic. the objective is to create us feel better By investing fair a small time each day centering on how to de-clutter our domestic, amid this clutter & organization challenge, we'll be able to have more peace in our domestic since we may feel way better around the space simply live in each day.

If we talk more conventionally, we see that getting freed of pointless things is as it were one half of the condition. Once you have got wrapped up de-cluttering, embrace a new approach to shopping. It can be troublesome at, to begin with, particularly on the off chance that you're enticed by modern items or convince yourself that something might come invaluable at an afterward date. For occurrence, in case you have got as of late cleared out your kitchen of unused cookware, you might feel compelled to purchase a few alluring unused ceramics while at the shopping center, fair since it looks great and since you presently have a few additional spaces. However, it's slippery incline – unless you check yourself, you'll conclusion up back where you started! If you cannot reasonably envision how you'll utilize an unused thing, don't purchase it. On the off chance that you know that you just wouldn't bother taking it with you when moving overseas, don't purchase it. You get the thought that makes a point of securing as it were what you genuinely require.

To conclude, I reach a point that we start to see how much calmer our domestic feels without clutter and mess all over the put. We take note of how much less demanding it is to select a furnish within the morning and how much more confident we are feeling once we cleanse and curate our wardrobe. We see how our heart and soul can breathe a bit less demanding once we contract our commitments down to as it were the fundamentals. We recognize how much way better our body feels and looks once we feed it with basic, entirety things. We discover we'll listen to ourselves think once more after we select to deliberately expand by unsubscribing, unfriending, and unfollowing. Sooner or afterward, these minutes of clarity and disclosure include up and we start to see that the ancient proverb "less is more" has a few genuine weight behind it. We begin to see the conceivable outcomes open to us when our life isn't continuously filled to flooding. We start to see fair how much you were lost when life was stuffed full of superfluous things, commitments, data, and concepts that included no genuine.

A little perspective I want to add here, the fundamental component isn't how we are doing it, what we keep, or the number of matters we subsequently wind up with. The necessary thing is permitting that cross in perspective fighting against the social message that the things we very own talk to our victory, merely should be busy to be profitable, that who we are and what we have bought will in no way be enough—and recognizing that the primary essential things in life have been never things.

CHAPTER THREE: DECLUTTER SERVICES TO RESCUE

De-cluttering is the removal of unnecessary items from non-public and public places which are overcrowded, disorganized and unpleasant and untidy. There are plenty of things to enjoy, to carry happiness, to deliver your self-coziness and calmness. De-cluttering is one of them and the most giant one as nicely. It is not constrained to the idea of bodily space however in addition to that we can relate it to the mental fitness as properly, while we get both the matters achieved collectively then they start increasing our cognizance and unfastened our thoughts to get matters done without pressure. We enjoy the lifestyle alongside the manner. So, cluttering can be something physical like books and garments with intellectual and emotions earlier. Anybody should observe that cluttered thoughts stay multidirectional and little matters get accomplished his imaginative and prescient gets blurred and cloudy as compared to other those who continue to be sharp just due to the fact. They don't have trouble as such. We can de-muddle the things in unique manners like we can de-clutter our friends, we can de-clutter our commitments, we can de-clutter our workplace, we can de-clutter our PC, we can de-clutter our domestics, and a lot more.

De-clutter services are being provided by many organizations in the world. We can have home organizers and personal organizers as well. The cost of home organizers varies from time to time. About 30 dollars to 8o dollars per hour are being offered but in case of personal organizers, 80 dollars to 130 dollars for personal organizers. It is a bit high in the case of personal organizers. An organization like "WEDECLUTTER" helps with a variety of different services from unpacking and organizing to creating files in the offices. It is much more possible that our lives may be hectic, stressful, busy and different from being straightforward but our homes don't need to. Life is all about ups and downs and causes a lot of pain and stress but those things which are in our control like de-clutter the cluttered things. A relaxing, pleasant, calm and organized space can help us to start our mornings start easier and welcoming. A good start is also a sign of fortunes as well. It is very common in many families that their things are not de-cluttered and when they wake up early in the morning they start placing their items in their places and waste a lot of their time because they do it every day without any proper management and direction. If they organize well their items, then it will not be hectic for them every morning but still, it is a good sign for them as they do it every day. I'm just pointing out that they should work in more efficient ways and time-saving ways rather than just rushing into all the time. But still, there are a lot of companies who offer their workers to de-clutter the items of houses, offices, etc. because for some people it is not that important and some other stuff being more important so they hire the workers from such organizations to manage their such small work.

Organizations and companies like "WEDECLUTTER" and there is a home consultant organization that I know, "The Tidy Lady". If we talk about "The Tidy Lady", this organization work for different categories like moving houses, downsizing, making kitchens more efficient and functional, to make the wardrobe gorgeously organized and practical storage as well. In the case of children which are the main reason for disorganizing the items of the beloved home, such companies can change the children's room into a less invigorating less centered space and a clean and alluring hangout. They can plan the child's capacity space with bespoke cabinetry or assist you to select and install basic capacity to form it simpler for us to oversee our child's toys and clothes. Less is unquestionably more! Let's declutter. When we tackle the space that scares us we'll go through our child's possession together and decrease them down to more sensible volume. Then compose what is cleared out to create it simple for us and our family to keep it looking clean and attractive.

When we talk about moving homes there may be many problems for us like packing, loading the luggage on to the trucks and then unloading the items and then again setting the new home that is the new and very difficult and time-consuming as well. They help us to make our homes presentable and better to the buyers by setting them by taking into consideration the likes and moods of buyers. They help us to present our home a dream and de-cluttered, spacious and inviting to the buyers. One of the reviews from the customers of the tidy lady said named A & H, WHANGAPAROA:

"Tidy Lady helped us "getting organized". We are moving house and didn't know where to start from. Our garage was in a messy state (Semi hoarding) and needed de-cluttering fast. Tidy Lady came to the rescue, Lizzie had a good starting point and a creative plan. She knew the steps to take starting with cleaning out the storage space first, then going through everything that needs to be stored to decide what to keep, then figure out how to best fit it in that space. My husband doesn't like at all to change and found the process a bit daunting, but Tidy Lady kept him focused and productive and made the whole process a lot easier to accomplish"

These organizations also work to make our kitchens more functional and efficient. everyone loves their kitchen people wrestles with pot and pans, straining to reach into that deep dark cupboard or on their knees trying to find that matching lid. Let's get your kitchen organized. They can make our kitchen easier to use, more efficient and more attractive. they can declutter, keeping only the things we use and need, and organize every single cupboard and drawer.

We and our family enjoy time in our kitchen so much more! It is easier to find what we need and to put things away because everything will have its place. They can also sort out office kitchens that are inefficient and make people grumpy. Old expired or unused makeup, expired sunscreen, expired medicine, old or ratty hair ties, broken brushes, old perfume, old toiletries, dried up nail polish, old and ratty toilets and mats all are the cluttered items in our home.

When we deal with the office, we have many other cluttered items like old books and magazines, old receipts coupons and papers, dried up pens and markers, outdated software and electronics, old batteries, chargers and cords, old paint cleaners and detergents, broken tools, unused DVD's and games, unused holiday items, and décor can come in office a mic category. When we talk about broken appliances then we come to know about expired food in the fridge, expired boxed and canned goods, unused or old cookbooks, ratty old dishtowels, and rags, broken appliances, chipped plates, bowls, and glasses, old kitchen utensils, and tools, broken or old jewelry, earrings with missing pies, ratty or stained clothes, unused purses or bags, clutter on and in nightstands, old shoeboxes, mismatched and missing socks, old ratty and stained bedding, etc these all things create a lot of mess and when we deal with them altogether or if not if we deal with them simultaneously then they create a lot of problems and issues in even families and relations when we mock each other when we aren't able to get anything and shout on each other then it results in many subsequent results. Firstly it looks a little time taking or a difficult and useless thing but it can solve a lot of issues that we don't even think about.

APDO (Association of Professional Declutterers & Organizers) perform unique things that usually amazes us. For example, moving to a smaller home: If we are overwhelmed by the thought of downsizing everything we own to fit a smaller house or a retirement apartment? It's always easier when we have a kind and caring, practical person to lend a helping hand. the organization will support us in making decisions about what to take with us, sensitively help with the selection of our much-loved belongings, making sure our furniture fits our new home and help with packing, unpacking and setting up our new home. It will be a weight off our shoulders to know that we don't have to do it on our own.

They help us to downsize like If we are worried about our mom and dad then It can be an emotional and upsetting time when a loved family member has to move. They let them take away some of the stress by helping us to make practical decisions and co-ordinate the move with sensible kindness. Together we can get so much more done and make the process so much easier. And there won't be any huge surprise bills or fee at the end and yes we can say it because you are giving them a huge work, someone who even don't know about your home settings before and still meeting the requirements of owners and it is a very amazing thing to appreciate and pay.

Imagine on foot into your cloth wardrobe and now not most effective finding precisely what we feel like wearing effortlessly and speedy but loving what we see? Does our wardrobe reflect who we are now or who we want to grow to be? A fantastically organized cloth cabinet is a satisfaction, whether it's ordered right into a rainbow of steeply-priced coloration, seasonal sleeve length or curated to reflect your dream of a character, minimal fashion.

In case we are beaten with the aid of the sheer volume of our clothes they can assist us to decide on what to hold, what to donate, and organize what's left so it's effortlessly easy to keep. Just need our wardrobe organized? No hassle, go and have espresso with your pals, they will get it looked after. We mustn't dispose of an aspect if all we need is an appropriate enterprise and a better way to discover what we need while we need it. their services are similarly to be had to those whose houses most effective want a minimal quantity of control. That's why we're often referred to as by using customers who are planning to sell and want to restore their residence to its most aesthetically attractive state ahead as well as people who truly need to open up their property and make it appear greater spacious. They are glad to work in any part of our own home. They recognize that everybody and assets are extraordinary can regularly emerge as stored in an array of places. From overflowing attics to storage rooms that are splitting on the seams, they can be able to free up a few areas and get everything looking spick and span once more.to get an assist anyone who wants their aid in de-cluttering their domestic and making their property a greater pleasant vicinity to live. Their professional members are dedicated to creating glad and comfortable accommodation for their customers. To analyze more about how they may help you, get in contact with them by filling forms or whatever requirements they usually demand.

In Pakistan, it is a bit different from other developed countries mostly. Not in all the cases but in most of the cases. People with their contacts or advertisements get mostly ladies who work for them accordingly form cleaning, washing of clothes or other household items to convert the cluttered house into de-cluttered one. A very less pay they get because they work from home to home. They usually don't work for only one house but in some cases, they also work for one house and even live with the family as well. A family takes care of her and her family by paying them and giving them their used items which are also another source to de-clutter the items. I conclude that it's an important issue and people are not aware of it. If they are not able to de-clutter by themselves, then seek help from organizations to get things done.

CHAPTER FOUR: DECLUTTER YOUR OFFICE

Sometimes, we simply feel tired of organizing stuff. We spend a lot of time organizing and re-organizing stuff that it uses up our time, and then we can't use that time to do the things we love. Purging our home or our office of unnecessary things is important. If you select to be more profitable and centered in your work, getting clutter out of your work range is basic. Research says that a cluttered desk of certain people is a sign of their genius and they have a lot of other things to do and there is a lot of stuff that is more important to them as compared to other things like clearing their rooms or offices. But one more point that must be pondered at that genius people work for the cause of people and solve unknowns, and they work for themselves as well but in offices, if you are working under your boss then there could be many other problems as well and a well de-cluttered office provide you an ease and relaxation with a fresh mind.

Why bother de-cluttering within the top priorities? There are a few benefits. To begin with, you'll spare space. Moment, a cleanroom or office can help concentration. Disregarding superfluous stuff and looking through untidy drawers and heaps takes up valuable mental vitality which can be channeled towards more beneficial tasks. Finally, in case you have got less belonging, you may spare time when it comes to cleaning and upkeep. Very essentially, the less you possess, the less time you may spend sorting out and re-organizing your domestic. In case you are feeling like clutter makes you're feeling overpowered, on edge, or upset… it's not in your intellect. Considers demonstrating that it has this effect on us. De-cluttering contains a domino effect on the superior living. A clutter-free environment permits you to perform assignments of everyday living more effectively since everything you would like is promptly accessible and inside reach. For illustration, on the off chance that your dishes are clean and legitimately put away, you're more likely to eat at domestic and appreciate cooking. On a more profound level, a clutter-free space moreover contributes to your well-being since you'll subconsciously feel like you're giving yourself with the next level of self-care. De-cluttering may moreover assist you to feel way better almost yourself since it's something of an achievement.

About de-cluttering, we must need to consider some important ideas. We need to question whether we are fulfilling them or not then there is a chance that our problems may result from such things. Like is this thing something I frequently use? If not, is this something that I adore and flashes joy? Could somebody else utilize it more than me? Can I get absent without having this in my life? When was the final time I utilized this? Am I keeping this out of commitment or expectation? Am I holding onto this since I think I ought to adore it? Am I sparing this fair in case I'll require it… sometime in the not so distant future, down the road? Do I have products of the same thing? Could something else I claim do the same work? On the off chance that your office is in turmoil, it likely reflects the chaos in your intuitive intellect, impeding your capacity to stay centered. Clutter moreover limits your capacity to prepare data. Decluttering your physical space can assist your declutter in your intellect. This frequently comes about in a cleansing experience, where you are feeling lighter and have more room to breathe. As you start to confine from material possessions and put more significance on individuals and encounters, you may sense a feeling of opportunity which can end up addictive.

Studies have shown that a cluttered office may cause a lot of problems for your brain to work, and it limits your creativity as well. Desk buried under a mountain of paperwork, sticky notes and yesterday's lunch containers, pens on the desk, slides remain ON, chairs and stools placed here and there these are the signs of cluttered offices. In case employees' desktops are disorganized and disheveled, it may be something their imaginative mojo. An untidy workspace causes them to be less beneficial. Other than clutter advancing hesitation, having to clean it all up afterward fair takes more time absent from the critical work you depend on your representatives to do. A mess can, moreover, be physically and candidly depleting. So whereas cleaning off your work area completely to handle an unused venture may feel strangely cathartic, advance a work culture of cleaning as you go, so that everybody can get their best work done now not afterward.

Living in a cluttered area can be rationally depleting considering that it's almost incomprehensible to dismiss errands that are cleared out unfinished. This makes consistent low-level stretch, which can drain us of vitality, produce sentiments of being overpowered, and certainly disable our safe framework over time. Stress and uneasiness can be brought on through a variety of things, and de-cluttering your home isn't the as it had been factor you ought to be doing to war these issues. But certainly in the match that it makes a distinction a small, it is something you simply ought to think about trying. A few representatives swear they flourish in chaos and perform superior in, the midst of, the mess. In truth, some think, affirm a chaotic work area has merits for a few specialists. Mental Science finds jumbled situations appear to motivate breaking free of convention, which can deliver new insights. So for pack rats, a cluttered office may be conducive to working environment delight. But be beyond any doubt that this state of inventive chaos may not work well for everybody, so it's imperative to find a pattern of cleanliness for your office. Occasional work area cleanings can moreover keep your office slick and from being a blemish to going by officials and interviewers. Plan time for workers to occasionally clear out stacks of ancient papers, diminish the measure of expensive heaps on their work area, and endeavor to put work staples like pens and paper clips in their legitimate place.

The key to keeping the most important boisterous workplaces from searching like a garbage pile is being proactive approximately cleanliness. For occasion, giving all people a non-public junk can show up as a terrific thought, but in the match that your cleansing group of workers as it has been coming as soon as a week, these repositories can make a stinky, obnoxious environment for those sitting shut them. Energize your laborers to require their nourishment squander to a centralized waste bin after every supper, and clarify how little endeavors like this may move ahead of the entire office.

Once you know what is gaining its keep in your office, isolated everything that remains within the office from the things you need to move (e.g., things you'll take domestic or that have a place in a supply closet) or provide away. Be ruthless, indeed along with your catch-all drawer. Do not keep what doesn't back your work or make you truly cheerful to see. You ought to be able to recognize the reason for every single thing in your space, and there shouldn't be copies. If there are things you cannot give, drop them off at your nearest reusing center. Consider these tips as you go: Digitalize what you'll. Pictures frequently can assist you to let go of indeed more physical merchandise, and items like trade cards can go absent once you include the individuals who given them as LinkedIn contacts. Items you got for complimentary at workshops or traditions can't compete with grants or certificates of achievement. All in one unit (e.g., scanner-printer-fax, tape, and post-it holder) can be major space savors.

For analyzing the items for rearranging, once you comprehend what is picking up its preserve in your office, restrained everything that stays inner the workplace fronts he things you desire to cross (e.g., things you may take household or that have a put in a supply closet) or provide absent. Be heartless, indeed besides your catch-all drawer. Don't preserve what would not have returned your work or make you cheerful to see. You acquired to be in a position to apprehend the reason for every single element in your space, and there should not be duplicates. Within the occasion that there are matters you can't deliver, drop them off at your closest reusing center. Consider these guidelines as you go: Digitalize what you can. Pictures in many instances can help you let go of absolutely extra bodily stock, and things like change cards can go truant once you incorporate the humans who give them as LinkedIn contacts. Things you obtained for complimentary at workshops or conventions can't compete with awards or certificates of accomplishment. All in one device (e.g., scanner-printer-fax, tape, etc.)

Your computer or laptop is a very important item in your office and the wires used for them in case of computers should be properly placed but if we avoid computers and use laptops it will leave a lot of space in the office because computer or PC covers a lot of space like it has several others items to work with like CPU, like keyboards, mouse, etc; which covers the floor and keyboard covers the desk portion, so if we use a laptop instead of computers, then it will generate a lot of easiness for us. This is about external cluttered things about computers in offices, but what about the interior of the computer. What we have installed on the computer!? Office computers or laptops usually are messed with a lot of files, presentations, office work, assignments, software, and a lot of other things. Naturally, we see our cluttered PC and have not been managed and organized with proper hands, then it makes ourselves sick. We get stuck in fixing the files and managing the files. Our desktop gets flooded with a lot of files, and if we don't create proper folders to put them all together, then they create a messy situation for us. There are many Softwares like PTC creo parametric, SolidWorks, Python, Visual Studio, Microsoft Office, Excel, and so on. Some software creates files in number, you always have to face them, properly manage them, and don't get panic. This shows the responsibility, carefulness, and well-directed attitude towards your professional life. If you can manage all the flooded things in the office, you are unstoppable. Whenever your boss visits you or other employees for presentations or other purposes, then if you have de-cluttered well it will be easy to convey without any obstructed mind. It also shows your positive attitude and positive approach to your profession. This may impress the boss as well. A well-organized employee has much more liking as compared to the ignoring ones. We can't even portray them as ignored ones, but it can be a possibility. In my perspective, a disorganized employee can suffer from a lot of mismanagement as compared to the owner of the de-cluttered office.

Taking the time to clean can be troublesome but science and brain research demonstrates that it is advantageous. Building the propensity to clean each morning is the hardest portion of the handle, but you'll rapidly see comes about, and your domestic will see clean all through the week. You'll too get a sense of fulfillment and resolve to boost achievement from each little assignment you total. And, most imperatively, without the stretch of having to spend hours cleaning, you'll be able to unwind and appreciate your time off. Once cleaning is on your calendar, consider yourself committed to the work. Blocking off time too guarantees that the cleaning exertion isn't getting to meddle with anything else, so you'll be able to feel less pushed approximately it and acknowledge it as a need.

CHAPTER FIVE: SIMPLE HABIT CHANGES TO OBSERVE DECLUTTER

Often you might find yourselves in situations where you feel your mind is a mess. Everything is happening all at once and you aren't able to comprehend a single thing. They say the first thing to do when decluttering your mind is to physically declutter the space that you live in. It is proven how having a clutter-free environment can positively affect your mental health.

Once you decide that you want to clear out and organize the space that you live in, one might feel overwhelmed as to how and where to start. Major tasks like these are not easy to start but once you do start, it's easy to use your work high and kind of ride the way to task completion and it's worth it. Clean and organized spaces help you to think clearly and have a calming effect.

This article is going to be all about how you can change simple tasks you do daily and incorporate some habits here and there in your daily routine which will eventually be contributing to your goal of home declutter. It might not be a good idea to suddenly disturb everything everywhere. Slow down, look around and select a place you want to start from. This would advisably be a place you spend most of your time in. It can be your bedroom, your study room, your living room or even your kitchen.

THE BEDROOM

Your bedroom majorly consists of your bed. A simple daily habit you need to practice spiritually is to make your bed every morning as soon as you get out of it. A made bed will instantly start to make your room look cleaner. The reason I advise for making your bed as soon as you wake up is that once you start your daily chores and are into the grind you may find it super easy to keep procrastinating making your bed. So the bed needs to be made first thing in the morning and you will find that there is not much left to do after that.

Another effortless daily habit to observe declutter would be to return a thing where it belongs after using it. This way you won't have random things lying at random places. This can include returning your makeup to their assigned boxes after you are done getting ready in the morning, keeping your nightdress where it belongs after removing it in the morning, not leaving your slippers haphazardly lying around when you change into your work shoes. Remember to not leave any wires lying around the room, keep your chargers in drawers after using them. Not leaving drawers and cupboards open after getting stuff you need will also contribute to giving your room an overall tidy appearance.

The closet is often the most cluttered part of one's room. This is also the place from which most of the potential declutter can take place by donating clothes you don't wear anymore. One might think that he has no outfit he does not wear but that's not true. All of us have articles of clothing lying in our closets we haven't touched in months. These may include odd things like a top, a hat, a pair of jeans, a pair of socks, a scarf or a belt. The best way to figure out which clothes you are not wearing is to turn the hangers in your closet the other way round after you have worn an outfit. This way by the end of the month the hangers that are still unturned are exactly the outfits you don't wear. Another way of getting to these clothes can be when you're taking out the season's clothes at the end of summer or winter and replacing them with the new season's clothes. Being very frank if there are clothes you haven't worn the entire season, you definitely will not wear them in the next season also. So you should take such clothes out and donate them, this will give the underprivileged new clothes to wear and give you more storage space in your closet and clothes won't come flowing out when you open your closet.

Everyone organizes differently so take out some time one day and clear out and organize one part of your closet and you can choose another shelf for another day you can spare some time. This way you won't have to take out 5 hours altogether one day and clean out your closet. A simple daily habit would be to fold your clothes neatly and keep them in their assigned piles after wearing them if you're putting them back in the closet and not in the laundry. Have separate shelves and separate spaces for different articles of clothing. Keep your undergarments in one drawer, socks in the other, keep your jeans in one pile and t-shirts in the other. This way you will easily find what you're looking for which will save you time in the morning.

THE KITCHEN

Kitchens tend to appear very untidy and cluttered. They will start appearing disorganized after you use them once so it is super important to develop habits that will keep your kitchen clean and clutter-free. The most important habit is so to wash the dish right after you eat, whether it's a single plate or cup, it hardly takes two minutes to wash a single dish but can take up to half an hour if you keep piling up the dishes and do them at one time. All you need are dishes piled up in the sink to make your kitchen automatically look filthy. So instead of piling up dirty dishes wash them right after using them.

Kitchen organization can be one hell of a task because there is just too much stuff to organize in the kitchen. Try keeping separate cupboards for your glasses, cups, plates, separate drawers for knives, for spoons, forks. This way it will be easier to find crockery and cutlery when you need it. Another simple habit to declutter your kitchen is to throw away jars and boxes after the product is finished if you're not planning to recycle them. Getting rid of things you don't need and will not use in the future but they will keep lying around untouched, causing clutter and using up space is the key when it comes to organizing and decluttering your house. So go ahead and throw away that empty jam bottle.

Another habit you can develop is to keep things where they belong right after using them while cooking. Cooking something in the kitchen can lead to an unmanageable mess after you're done. It's easier to keep the salt back in the cupboard after you've added it than to leave it lying there and then keep the salt, pepper, vegetables, plates, sauces and other things away all at once after cooking. It's a good idea to keep your kitchen counters and stoves clean. It will help in achieving that overall neat appearance.

Even in the kitchen, you need to get rid of things that don't work anymore, things that are of no use to you anymore or extras, and you have never used them. Getting rid of these useless things will help make more space and generally declutter your kitchen shelves and cabinets.

THE STUDY

A clear and decluttered workspace is proved to be an integral part of the motivation you need to study and get things done. I cannot emphasize enough on the importance of decluttering your workspace, which includes the entire environment that you work in, your study desk, your bookshelves, your drawers, and cabinets. Your energy when you're working at a cluttered desk is very different from when you're working on an organized and tidy desk. Make sure you keep only the supplies you need for doing that specific task you're working on the desk. Anything extra will lead to distraction and unnecessary clutter. Organize the books on your bookshelf. Setting height-wise is a good idea. Decluttering your bookshelves is very important. Removing books, you've outgrown or don't need anymore will free the space you need for new books because you should keep learning throughout life. Get rid of random things that you don't need to work or study from the room since it's your workplace it should only have things you need to work. A simple habit you can develop in this regard can be returning everything on your desk that was there for a specific task to their assigned drawer, cabinet or shelf after you're done with that specific task so that you don't have irrelevant stuff lying on your desk when you plan to do something else.

LIVING ROOM

It's the main room of the house, it's the last place that should be a cluttered mess. Your living room should always be tidy and decluttered because you relax there, you invite guests in there. You never know when someone can show up unexpectedly. A habit you can develop in this regard is to keep the sofa cushions where they belong after you get up from there, keep your TV remote at one assigned place so you don't need to search the entire house for the remote control when you wish to watch television. Remove stuff that does not belong to the living room from the living room. You don't want toys and plates lying around the living room. It's always a good idea to have good fragrances to fix your vibes.

THE BATHROOM

You should clean and wash your bathroom daily. I repeat, daily. A good habit to keep your washroom organized and decluttered is to throw away empty bottles of products you have used, shampoos, conditioners, skincare, and everything. There's no use of empty containers and bottles lying around the bathroom, cluttering it and taking up space. You should keep your washroom dry and a good habit is to dry it right after you shower as opposed to leaving it wet and then spending extra time while cleaning it. Time is money, time is precious so every habit you develop should be using it wisely.

THE STOREROOM

Okay, I admit that most of us just dump all the clutter from the entire house into the storeroom, but decluttering the storeroom is also important because one day you'll open your storeroom and it will be humanly impossible to clear it then because then it will be overflowing. You can do this less often than you spend on the rest of the house but maybe an annual storeroom declutters or a six-month storeroom declutter is healthy. When you do plan to clear out your storeroom the things to do are to remove everything you don't need right now and won't be needing shortly. A good habit for making your annual storeroom declutter easier is to figure out whether or not you need this certain thing in the future there and then and not throwing it into the storeroom unnecessarily if you don't need it in your life anymore. It's as simple as that. If you have figured out you don't need a certain thing then throw it out of your house instead of throwing it into your storeroom. Your storeroom or attic should be the room in your house that you should use for actually storing stuff you might not need in a specific season or a specific part of the year but you know you would need to take it out in another season or for storing out of season clothes or lawn machinery and other things you don't want in plain sight.

Life is not easy, you have to make life easy by many coping mechanisms and to declutter the physical space that you live in which is ultimately going to lead to decluttering of your mind is a good, effective and healthy start. Happy decluttering!

CHAPTER SIX: ENVIRONMENT & COGNITIVE ABILITY

Do you feel challenged once you attend work? Does one feel as if your work environment is clean and organized? Does your environment you're working in effect your discernment?

This chapter covers the consequences of the environment on your brain's ability to know things around you and your sagacity. Often you would possibly end up in a situation where you're unable to gauge things quite effectively when the environment in which you're working isn't well organized and methodical. Your brain might feel suffocated and irritated by things around you albeit this stuff is of use.

The environment indeed features a great impact over your thinking and comprehensive abilities either it's an office or a classroom. The human brain is easier where the items around it are in an orderly fashion and systematic. Your brain's comfort is the base of your understanding level. The clean and unsullied environment provides A level of satisfaction and appeasement to your brain. Happiness is directly associated with your brain's health. And the brain's health is directly associated with your cognitive abilities. Whether it is your office, studies or creativity, your success depends on your brain's health and its discernment.

A study at Florida State University shows that the individuals who are exposed to a piece of the environment that's untidy and spoiled may very well affect your brain negatively. Both a scarcity of stimulation within the workplace and a feculent environment can have a long-term effect on employees.

"Psychologists say that the brain may be a muscle, while industrial hygienists point to chemicals within the work environment which will cause decline," –Joseph Grzywacz, the Norejane Hendrickson Professor of Family and Child Sciences and lead researcher on the study.

Your environment contains factors that will sculpt your cognitive abilities. Some of which you'll touch, see and other you can't. Both of those things interest your mental and cognitive health. Within the past researchers had been divided on whether it had been a tidy and unclean workplace – exposure to loud noises or chemicals like lead or working during an unstimulating workplace that took the most important toll on people's cognitive health as they age. Both of those issues play an important role in affecting the mental and cognitive health of workers and employees. Long-term exposure to the bad and unclean environment can cause cognitive decline and may cease creativity in adults.

Great companies and industries have their offices well organized and clean. They supply their employees with the best environment to urge them to work on higher efficiencies. That's the rationale of why great companies become more and more successful. Employee's cognitive abilities are enhanced in this way, and they are ready to work quite efficiently in a clean environment. Cognitive decline is a major issue globally. To eradicate it, companies are designing jobs that each one of the workers may have some deciding abilities by providing them with a healthy and clean environment.

Cognitive abilities are key competencies that are needed to satisfy the challenges of job demands, education, and advanced training, societal expectations, and therefore the demands of the lifestyle of middle-aged adults. Middle adulthood provides many good opportunities for creating intellectual contributions, given the position of middle-aged adults within the family, workplace, and society. Hence, middle-age is the period of the highest performance in a variety of individual domains. Middle-aged adults typically perceive themselves or are perceived by others as having not only more status and responsibility but also simpler intelligence and integrative skills.

Education, in its broadest sense, maybe a process designed to inculcate knowledge, skills, and attitudes necessary to enable individuals to cope effectively with their environment. Its primary purpose is to foster and promote the fullest individual self-realization for all people. It's indispensable to normal living, without education the individual would be unqualified for group life. Education is the process of developing the capacities and potentials of the individuals to prepare that individual to achieve success during a specific society or culture. Notably, it's often said to be a powerful tool for developing intellectual abilities, shaping cultural attributes, acquiring knowledge and skills also as a favorable tool to maneuver a nation towards developing its scientific and technological culture. Achieving this goal requires an understanding of commitment to the proposition that education may be a primary instrument for the social and economic advancement of human welfare.

Academic performance is often mentioned because of the level of performance at college and grade. And it's indeed the bottom of educational growth and universal concepts. It's estimated that genes contribute about 20–40% of the variance in intelligence in childhood and about 80% in adulthood. Thus, the environment and its interaction with genes account for a high proportion of the variation in intelligence seen in groups of young children, and for a little proportion of the variation observed in groups of mature adults. The stress of status and widest responsibilities may encourage the event of those intellectual skills. For instance, diverse work environments and workplace conditions may contribute to job-specific and individual differences within the development of cognitive abilities. As such, the event of cognitive abilities is more strongly influenced by environmental factors compared to other developmental periods.

The environment features a great impact on the student's academic performance and cognitive abilities. Humans continue learning their whole life but the foremost important learning stage is between 10 and 30 age. Learning and growing directly relates to the environment we sleep in. Students in schools and colleges enhance their cognitive abilities but as long as they facilitated with a far better and tidy environment. It is sensible that students would do better once they learn in positive environments. After all, most people would agree that some environments are more conducive to learning and academic performance. A student taking a test during a quiet, peaceful room will almost certainly do better than a student taking an equivalent test during a loud, chaotic room.

Just because something is sensible, however, doesn't mean that educators and policymakers have the knowledge they have to form better decisions that will help students reach their goals. Now that this study has revealed how some factors affect students, educators can begin making changes that will improve learning environments.

The study also shows what proportion influence environments wear student success. Its findings show that students who learn in positive environments effectively receive a month and a half more math instruction than those in poor learning environments.

The same research paper shows that positive learning environments can lower teacher turnover by 25 percent. This is often significant because teacher turnover has been linked to increased costs and poor student achievement. Schools that provide better environments, in other words, could potentially reach higher levels of success while spending less money.

Students develop a better level of intellectual abilities and become more creative by learning in an unsullied environment. In the meantime, parents can use this information to create an optimum environment reception. This optimum environment reception is often achieved by decluttering and removing off useless stuff. This makes our house spacious, during this way our brain doesn't feel suffocated and stifle. The human brain works better during a well-organized environment, so parents can take several steps like these to make an interesting environment reception to reinforce the cognitive abilities of their children. Study shows that spacious environment helps our brain to relax and work on its best condition. Thus, the academic performance of scholars is increased by facilitating them with this sort of environment. Proper and well-ordered school rooms are recommended by a psychologist to stay a student's brain calm and relaxed. Moreover, classrooms are painted in different colors and decorated with charts to develop an interesting environment for college kids. This enchanting description of a classroom at the fictional Hogwarts School of Witchcraft and Wizardry captures three fundamental ideas from the environmental psychology of teaching and learning.

First, all learning takes place during a physical environment with quantifiable and perceptible physical characteristics. Whether sitting during a large lecture hall, underneath a tree or ahead of a display screen, students are engulfed by environmental information. Specific targets within the environment draw the students' attention, like armchairs, scarves, and teacups, and that they continuously monitor the ambient properties like the sunshine of the lamps, the smell of the kettle, and therefore the warmth of the hearth. In any learning environment students are awash in environmental information, only a little fraction of which constitutes the sights and sounds of instruction.

Second, students don't touch, see, or hear passively; they feel, look, and listen actively. Students cannot attend to all or any the environmental information bombarding them at any given time; their ability to collect and understand incoming information is restricted. Through automatic and standardized processes, students usually select information for consideration. They struggle to know what they're sensing by piecing bits of data together from rock bottom up and by applying existing thoughts and preconceptions from the highest down. A classroom with circular tables and cozy armchairs may look strange because it deviates from expectations formed through prior experience. Students may direct their attention to particular targets within the learning environment that they find more interesting, important, or unfamiliar than others. For some, it'd be the instructor's engaging chemistry demonstration. For others, it's going to be the silvery ball on the shelf. In any learning environment, students manage their cognitive skills by actively selecting environmental information for further consideration and by using existing knowledge structures to interpret this information in ways in which have worked previously.

Third, the physical characteristics of learning environments might affect learners emotionally, with important cognitive and behavioral consequences. Although emotional reactions to environmental stimuli are shown to vary widely across individuals and activities, most students would probably find learning difficult during a stiflingly warm classroom. Conversely, environments that elicit positive emotional responses may lead not only to enhanced learning but also to a strong, emotional attachment there to space. It's going to become an area where students like to learn, an area they hunt down once they wish to find out, and an area they remember fondly once they reflect on their learning experiences. In education, we hope to supply such places for our students to find out, whilst we build yet one more large lecture hall and plan to squeeze our students into crowded, noisy, and uncomfortable spaces. Some learning environments are easier and offer fewer distractions than others. In any learning environment, physical characteristics that cause discomfort are often expected to interfere with learning; environments that produce positive emotional states are often expected to facilitate learning and therefore the development of place attachment. The areas of psychology that relate most to classroom design and learning environments are environmental, educational, human factors (engineering), and psychology. Previous research on the consequences of such environmental variables as light, temperature, and noise on learning has yielded some predictable results that are addressed through traditional classroom design. Learning appears to be affected adversely by inadequate light, extreme temperatures, and loud noises—variables maintained within acceptable ranges in most college classrooms. Other results, however, reflect the usually complex, subtle, and surprising interplay between the learner and therefore the learning environment. Years of research about the effects of environmental variables on human thoughts, feelings, and behaviors indicate that other variables often moderate the consequences of environmental variables. During a summary of the research on educational environments, Weinstein[2] concluded that environmental variables can impact learners indirectly which the consequences of various physical settings often depend upon the character of the task and therefore the learner.

It can be summarized that the character of the environment we live in features a great impact on the cognitive abilities of our brain. A clean and tidy environment proves to be optimal for working while on the opposite hand the sullied environment damps our discernment. To enhance one's cognitive ability, one must organize his workplace as well as his home to achieve maximum comfort in his mind. Decluttering would be a better and easier option.

CHAPTER SEVEN: DIFFERENT WAYS TO DECLUTTER YOUR HOUSE OR OFFICE

When is clutter a problem? For several people clutter is often an energy zapper or they waste inordinate amounts of your time trying to find things they can't find. In extreme cases, people may suffer from obesity or depression when a lifetime of consumption extends beyond "stuff". In hoarding situations, a house filled with clutter can cause fire hazards and other health complications when mold and mud are present. But extreme cases aren't common.

What is clutter? Clutter is anything you're keeping around your house that doesn't add value to your life. Decluttering is all about making room in your home for the items that matter. Why do you have to declutter?

Many of us enjoy decluttering because it relieves stress by providing a way of control and accomplishment. For others, getting obviates the junk frees up a touch extra space within the house that wasn't there before. Some people may get to purge before they move to a replacement house. Whatever your reasons for decluttering your life and/or residential property are, this guide will assist you through the method "Excessive clutter" which is usually a symbol and an explanation for stress and may affect every facet of your life: from the time it takes you to try to things to your finances and your overall enjoyment of life. Clutter can distract you, weigh you down and generally it brings chaos into your life.

Whether you tackle it as a part of downsizing effort or just to simplify your life, decluttering a whole house is an enormous job. The best thanks to tackling it's in stages—to specialize in one room, one space, or maybe one zone within an area (like your kitchen cabinets), completing the work fully before moving on to the next space. This will also build confidence as you experience visible success at each step.

To start with decluttering, you have to follow some simple steps:

- Write down or make a map of all the rooms and 'clutter hot spots' you would like to tackle.
- Give each space a grade that supported the severity of the clutter. For instance, on a scale of One-to-Three, (3 being the foremost cluttered), a very messy room or closet would

get a 3. this may assist you to prioritize some time.

- Do one room or one space at a time.
- Set completion dates for every phase of your cleanup. Make certain to select dates that are attainable so you don't get frustrated. If you create it into a, declutter challenge for yourself, it's going to feel a touch more sort of a game.
- In addition to completion dates, you ought to plan time to figure on specific areas once you expect to declutter those spaces to require longer than a couple of hours, like a basement or a garage.

You don't need fancy tools to declutter your home, but you do need five baskets or bins defined for these five purposes:

1. <u>Put Away</u>: This container is for items that have crept out of their storage spaces. This could mean a cup within the bathroom or a sweatshirt within the kitchen. These are items that will go back to their designated spots.

2. <u>Recycle</u>: This bin is for items that need to be recycled, such as paper, plastic or glass. Recyclable glass, plastics, and paper can go straight into your bin if you've got a curbside pickup. Otherwise, put your recyclables in bags, so you'll transport the waste to the closest recycling drop off location.

3. <u>Fix, Mend</u>: Use this container for items that need further tinkering, such as a pair of shoes that you love but which need to be cleaned.

4. <u>Trash</u>: Designate one basket for items that are simply trash—things that can go into the household trash immediately. 5. Have a Garage Sale: If you're up to the task, you'll be ready to make touch money off your clutter by having a yard sale. Check to ascertain if your neighborhood or homeowner's association features a designated yard sale date. Just confirm you start your decluttering process early enough so you'll participate – you'll get more pedestrian traffic that way.

5. <u>Donate</u>: Designate one bin for items that you can donate to a charitable organization or another person. These should be items you can imagine another person wanting or needing. You can use bins, baskets or maybe just cardboard boxes for this task. You can

bring these bins into each room as you declutter or leave them in a central place in your home while you work. The important thing is that you don't go hunting for containers while you're decluttering—set up the bins before you begin.

Tart with your medicine cabinet. Take everything out and discard exprired medications, makeups, and skincare products. Put everything you're keeping immediately back into the cabinet, storing the items you use most often at eye level. Next, move onto any cabinet drawers. Remove everything, do a fast evaluation of what you're keeping and what you're tossing. Put the items you're going to keep back into their drawers, with the items you use most often in the top drawers.

Now, do the same process with your shower, tub. Finally, pull everything out from below your bathroom sink and declutter the things there. Finally, everything that did not have a home can be quickly sorted into the five baskets or bins you have staged for the purpose. first, make your bed. It's hard to feel any progress decluttering a bedroom while an unmade bed stares you in the face. Start with your nightstands and remove anything on them that doesn't belong there and put it in your "Put Away" bin. This may include books, newspapers and magazines you have already finished reading, broken eyeglasses, pens and paper, and mail. Throw out or recycle anything that you no longer use, such as empty tissue boxes, pens that have gone dry, or chargers that no longer work. Do the exact process with the tops of your dressers, chests, and, or bureaus. Pay careful attention to any clothing that is strewn about. Anything that needs folding or hanging goes into the Put Away bin. If you're afraid it's going to wrinkle further, you'll lay clothes down on your bed.

You don't need to attend the shop to shop for something. You'll use small gift boxes, shoe boxes, cereal boxes or repurpose plastic containers to carry the things within the drawer. Get creative – perhaps you won't need to send as many things to the landfill at the top of the day! Go through each bureau, drawer by drawer. Take everything out. Pull out anything that's not worn and put it in your Donation bag or box. Fold and store everything you're keeping. If you retain a desk or vanity table in your bedroom, tackle that next. Resist the urge to shove things back to drawers, instead, put them in your Put Away bin. Toss or recycle any garbage or anything you haven't used in more than six months. Return items to their proper places. Fold or hang and store any clothing. If you're now eyeing your closet, don't worry—we'll tackle that next! It's time to tackle your closet. The easiest way to declutter a closet is to start from decluttering your clothing by type. That means start with shoes, then boots dresses, then denim, etc. It's much easier to decide to toss or keep a pair of jeans if you're watching your entire jean collection directly. So start coitus interruptus differing types of clothing and choose what you'll toss and keep. Once you've skilled each sort of clothing, you'll have four piles to deal with:

- Put away anything that was simply in the wrong spot. Example: If you had a pair of socks in your closet, put them in your dresser.
- Put any dirty laundry into the hamper or bring it to the laundry room.
- Anything that needs to be repaired should go to the tailor or dry cleaner.
- Donations and consignments go to a donation center or a consignment store (either online or a brick and mortar outlet).
- You may not have a traditional mudroom or foyer, but you have an entryway. No matter how small it is, the best way to make an entryway most functional is to declutter it regularly.
- Start with any desk, console, or side tables you have in your entry. Go through each drawer, removing the contents and make a fast decision to toss or keep each item. Go over the tops of each desk or console as well.

Do you have a space for your keys and other important items? Make sure everything is accessible and not too crowded. This will make it easier to leave the house with what you need each morning.

- The hall closet should be decluttered like any other closet: Start with shoes and boots, then jackets, followed by accessories.
- The entry is another area that picks up tons of clutter from other rooms. Spend time putting away things from other rooms that have made it's thanks to the entry.
- Keeping your kitchen clutter-free is often a challenge because numerous different activities occur there—cooking, eating, and socializing. As a result, the kitchen has many various sorts of items stored in it. You'll prefer to declutter your kitchen by focusing one category of an item at a time (cutting boards, glassware, utensils or bakeware, for example) or going by zone through each a part of the kitchen.
- The initiative is to empty each space, assess each item, and put everything back where it belongs. Start together with your powerhouse storage spaces first, like the pantry and upper cabinets. Then move onto the lower cabinets, drawers, the space under the sink.

- Finally, consider your countertops. Move as many items as possible off of the countertops and into storage spaces. Keep only what you employ every single day on the countertops.

- Finally, take your Put Away bin and return anything that does not belong within the kitchen to its rightful space for storing elsewhere within the house. The front room is one of the toughest rooms in your home to stay neat on a day today. That's because it gets tons of use and living rooms don't usually offer tons of storage features. You'll have some bookcases and a TV console, but they don't hide much. The key's to:

- Decide on permanent storage spaces for commonly used items like remote controls, magazines, and books.

- Declutter this space regularly. Start with bookcases, console, and side tables. Then move onto your cocktail table and wall unit. Empty them, assess the things they store then return them to their proper storage spaces.

Put books away, action your mail, return remote controls to their proper places, fold blankets, etc. Move onto electronics. Remove everything that's not connected to your television or home theatre system. Are you using it? Does it work? Store items like chargers, gadgets, and gaming equipment where you employ them. Finally, tackle the toys. Assess every toy to wear and tear. Does it still function? Do your kids still play with it? Recycle or store each toy. Grab your Put Away bin and return everything that belongs in another room to its proper space for storing. And avoid buying useless stuff because it only covers space. Also, you place small garbage buckets in each room and clear them out in the morning daily.

Once you create many order and harmony in your home, you'll be more present and radiant. Principle and every one of Traditional Chinese Medicine mention the circulation of vital force energy because of the key to vibrant health and abundance. Like acupuncture, which removes blockages and imbalances from the body to make more dynamism and wellness, clearing clutter removes blocks and imbalances from your space. once you move through spaces that are lit up with fresh energy, inspiration strikes and therefore the most magnetic parts of your personality can come to life. These small steps are your way to happiness.

CHAPTER EIGHT: EFFECTS OF CLUTTERING & DECLUTTERING

Decluttering is that the process whereby you opt whether the things in your space are clutter and if not, decide where they belong, and action that calls. The process will help you make a permanent change by enabling you to understand why you have clutter in the first place.

Decluttering imposes a great impact on our daily life. It affects in many ways which we will be discussing in this chapter. According to science decluttering has the greatest effect on our mental and physical health. Our relationships with family and other people are also affected by this even though we do not think much about it.

Clutter can cause feelings of stress, fatigue, and depression, consistent with recent research. We've evolved a preference for order and symmetry because presumably, those things conferred an evolutionary advantage back in our ancestral environment. When things check out of order, it can (but not always do) make us feel scattered and anxious.* Creating order relieves that anxiety. A University of California study found that levels of the strain hormone cortisol were higher in mothers who lived in homes they described as "cluttered" or filled with "unfinished projects. Stress contributes to poor sleep, poor eating habits and general poor health, so it is a good idea to start out decluttering – One step at a time. Put aside quarter-hour per day to draw up one place, like a messy shelf or drawer. This manner you'll feel happier and more relaxed at the top of the day, and gradually create more order as you go along. Since decluttering reduces stress, you'll naturally enjoy better sleep. But keeping your bedroom decluttered is itself an aid to sleep. People who take the time to form their beds every morning experience longer, more restful sleep, especially once they use fresh, clean sheets. Decluttering one's bedroom should also include keeping electronic devices turned off or in another room, so you can unwind and go to sleep at an earlier hour. (And by staying more organized during the day, there will be fewer tasks to distract you later.)

Clutter is visually distracting. The sheer number of objects in your field of vision can affect your ability to consider one thing at a time, albeit you think that you're multitasking efficiently. Consistent with a study by the Princeton Neuroscience Institute, clutter overloads the visual area and interferes with its ability to process information. Once you cut the clutter, you can think and work efficiently, thus enabling you to spend less time on tasks, both reception, and the work. Doing so leaves you with longer for enjoying personal activities, longer to spend with family, longer to organize healthy meals, and longer to rest. It's hard to specialize in important tasks when several things compete for your attention. Researchers have found that being around disorganization makes it harder for your brain to focus. It is often especially tough for people with ADHD (attention deficit hyperactivity disorder). If you've got ADHD, a knowledgeable organizer or coach could also be the simplest thanks to restoring some order to your space.

The stress triggered by your clutter can also trigger coping mechanisms like overeating "comfort foods," consistent with a Cornell University study. A psychological experiment conducted at the University of Minnesota likewise found that while disorder can sometimes spur creativity, a messy room was more likely to steer to eating unhealthy snacks than eating healthy ones. Within the latter study, people that hung out in an unorganized room were twice as likely to eat chocolate candy than an apple. While there could also be multiple reasons why people eat more poorly in cluttered surroundings, it's an honest idea to form cooking and dining areas as free from clutter as possible.

Along with triggering poor food choices, science shows that clutter can cause weight gain, too. A study conducted by researchers at Florida State University has revealed a link between hoarding and obesity, noting that folks with extremely cluttered homes were 77 percent more likely to be overweight. While not everyone features a severe hoarding problem, clutter-linked weight gain can also point to people's too-busy lifestyles. Individuals during a rush are more likely to eat what's handy, like pre-packaged and fast foods, which successively causes obesity. During a more organized home, there's longer to plan and prepare healthier meals – also as longer to relax and eat more slowly.

There's a reason people often call knickknacks "dust collectors. An excessive amount of stuff makes it harder to stay your space clean. If you're allergic to things like dust mites or pet dander, decluttering should make it easier to dust and vacuum and obtain symptoms like sneezing, wheezing, and itchy eyes in check. A clean tidy and decluttered home is vital for asthmatics and other people who suffer from pollinosis. Unfortunately, sometimes clutter enters our home and it's time to wash it up. If you've got an extreme sensitivity to dust and mud mites to declutter a touch at a time to scale back exposure. Get help together with your closet because clothing items are notorious for attracting dust and mud mites.

Removing off the waste material and dusty stuff from your house will help you with your allergy and hypersensitivity. Some people that sleep in cluttered homes have a poorer "working memory," consistent with research. Your brain is wired to be ready to keep track of only a couple of details directly for a brief period, so it can get overloaded when there's an excessive amount of happening. If you struggle to recollect names and numbers or frequently fail to follow the plot of a movie, help might be at hand. Scientists say the matter is that you simply got to declutter or spring-clean your mind. Experiments show that the memory lapses that accompany age aren't simply thanks to the brain slowing down. Instead, they will be blamed on the well-used brain finding it more and harder to prevent irrelevant information interfering with the task in hand. Organizing your environment will be very effective in keeping your mind calm and retaining your judging abilities.

A neat, tidy house feels inviting, both for the people that live there also as guests. A cluttered home may feel the other. But shutting people out can take a toll on relationships and cause you to feel sad and lonely. That would be one reason a hoarding disorder tends to overlap with depression and anxiety disorders.

Living with many clutter puts you in danger of getting injured. When your floor is roofed with boxes, tons of clothing, or maybe an excessive amount of furniture, it's that much easier to trip. Shelves stuffed to the brim with books and knickknacks also can be a hazard if something falls off or a bit of overloaded furniture topples over.

A more organized environment may cause you to more caring toward others. In one study, volunteers who filled out surveys during a neat room were more likely to mention they wanted to donate to a charity compared with those that were questioned during a messy room.

If you've gone overboard on papers and other flammable items, your home is often a fireplace hazard. Albeit a fireplace starts within the commonest of the way (Cooking oil goes up in flames, or a burner catches the sting of your dish towel.), clutter makes it harder to urge help. Not only will you've got more trouble getting the call at a time if your pathways and exits are blocked, but firefighters also will have a harder time putting out the blaze.

Smoke alarms, you might not be alerted to a fireplace if you've got too few of them or they're too distant. Put them on every level of the house, inside each bedroom, and just outside any bedroom areas, too. Experts recommend that you simply connect your smoke alarms so when one pops, all of them do. That helps if someone features a hearing problem, has headphones or earbuds on, or is doing something noisy (like employing a hairdryer). Smoke alarms aren't intended to inform you where the hearth is -- and remember, fire can spread quickly - but to warn you to urge out ASAP. Test smoke alarms once a month, change the batteries every 6 months and replace each device every 10 years.

The painkillers in your medicine chest are often risky. There is a chance you or someone in your family can get addicted or have an overdose. Never take quite your doctor to tell you and do not share with people. Keep your pills locked away and hidden from sight. Ask your doctor about the proper thanks to getting obviate extras.

A lot of house fires start on a snug couch. Smoking while you're lounging around may be a common cause. Lookout with cigarettes, pipes, and cigars, also as candles, space heaters, and lighters, especially when kids are around. This fungus puts tiny spores into the air which will cause breathing problems, asthma, and other allergies. It loves fresh foods, plants, and damp areas like basements, sinks, toilets, and bathtubs. Clean the kitchen often, especially refrigerator bins and seals. Quickly fix any leaks in your home. Wash fresh fruits and veggies before you set them away and throw them out before they begin to urge moldily.

The environment indeed features a superb impact over your thinking and comprehensive abilities either it's an office or a classroom. The human brain is easier where the items around it are in an orderly fashion and systematic. Your brain's comfort is that the bottom of your understanding level. The clean and unsullied environment provides A level of satisfaction and appeasement to your brain. Happiness is directly associated with your brain's health. And the brain's health is directly associated with your cognitive abilities. Whether it in your office, studies or creativity, your success depends on your brain's health and its discernment.

Do you shop around your home and wonder how it got so filled with knickknacks, or scan your office and ask yourself how it needs to be so buried in neglected piles of paper? What about your calendar: Is it crammed with appointments stretching indefinitely into the future? Is your email box so overflowing that you simply don't even desire wading in to undertake to deal with any but the most important emergencies?

All of this clutter, physical and mental, can interrupt your flow—both your ability to maneuver and your ability to think. It seems that your well-being could also become victim to what we'd call the "clutter effect. A set of recent studies on stress, life satisfaction, physical health, and cognition all speak to the worth of streamlining. If you're unable to urge through the fabric clogging up your neural networks, therefore the theory goes, you'll be slower and less efficient in processing information. As a result, you'll be incapacitated when it involves difficult tasks, and even in longer-range mental exercises once you need to come up with the information you ought to know, like names of individuals, that you simply can not find within your disorganized repository of data.

Streamlining seems to possess its advantages, then, not even as a housekeeping tool, but as an important process for maintaining your happiness in your home environment and at work. At an equivalent time, cutting through the clutter can benefit your physical health and cognitive abilities. Start getting out that trash bag, whether virtual or physical, and you'll soon feel better ready to enjoy your surroundings while you think that more efficiently and cleanly. A clean and tidy environment eliminates restlessness from our mind and body as well and we become more capable and efficient in doing a task or planning something. A healthy environment is necessary for a healthy life and only we can build an environment like this by removing off the useless stuff from our lives and homes.

CONCLUSION

In the light of the above evidence and facts, it can be concluded that decluttering is super essential to bring peace and calm in your life. This not only helps you in organizing yourself, but your workload, and stress. All you need is a mindset and effort.

If you are unable to declutter your house, or if you are busy, then you can hire services that will help you in organizing your house and getting rid of the excessive unnecessary material.

The above quotations and research will prove to be very beneficial for the people to observe decluttering. The habit changes can help the person in bringing positivity and growth in his lifestyle. In my opinion, decluttering home should be done by everybody as it plays a very vital role in your personality building. If you are tidy and neat all the time, then you have a strong, beautiful personality.

Happy Decluttering!

PERSONAL NOTES